30 ft.

END LINE

GOAL LINE

right end
right tackle
right guard
center
left guard
left tackle
left end

right halfback
quarterback
fullback
left halfback

50   40   30   20   10   END ZONE

On a professional field, the goalposts are set up on the goal lines, instead of the end lines, and the posts are closer together.

The playing area is marked off with white lines every five yards. These lines, which are made by spreading powdered lime, make the field look like a huge griddle. This is why the field is sometimes called the "gridiron."

Two dotted lines, also made with powdered lime, run from goal line to goal line. They are called the inbounds lines. The ball must always be put into play between these lines.

Four exciting stories of gridiron daring feature men whose very names—Len Dawson, "Super Joe" Namath, Otto Graham, and Steve Owen—mean the best in football. Each is portrayed at the peak of his career, leading his team to glory in a spectacular upset victory.

Written especially for the young reader's enjoyment are two action-packed Super-bowl replays. In 1969 the Minnesota Vikings were heavy favorites, but Kansas City Chiefs' quarterback "Lenny the Cool" Dawson beat the odds and stopped them cold. In an equally startling upset the next year, the Baltimore Colts tried to blitz the Jets' cocky wonder boy, Joe Namath. But when the final gun sounded the underdog Jets were amazingly number one.

Here are two other stunning upset games that fans will never forget. In 1950 Otto Graham of the fledgling Cleveland Browns was pitted against the Philadelphia Eagles' deadeye passer Tommy Thompson. Teamwork and superior strategy gave the Browns an unexpected win.

In 1934 the injury-plagued New York Giants didn't stand a chance against the mighty Chicago Bears. But in one of the most memorable comebacks in football history, coach Steve Owen's team won on a frozen field with a secret weapon —sneakers.

GEORGE SULLIVAN is a sports fan extraordinary. He writes, for General Features Corporation, a daily and weekly sports instruction column which appears in newspapers throughout the country. In more than a dozen books he has transmitted his enthusiasm and knowledge of hockey, bowling, billiards, golf, boxing, swimming, and football.

Born in Lowell, Massachusetts, he went to Fordham University in New York City where he still lives with his wife and son.

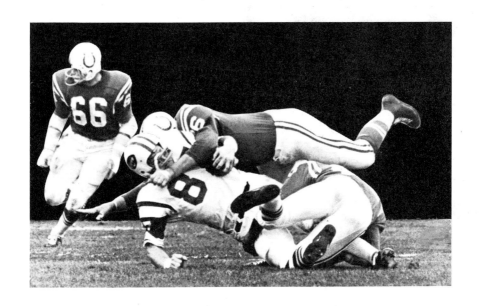

PRO
FOOTBALL'S
GREATEST
UPSETS

BY GEORGE SULLIVAN

GARRARD PUBLISHING COMPANY
CHAMPAIGN, ILLINOIS

Sports Consultant:
COLONEL RED REEDER
Former Member of the West Point Coaching Staff
and Special Assistant to the West Point
Director of Athletics

Photo credits:

Brown Brothers: p. 79 (top)
Culver Pictures: p. 71
The New York Times: pp. 34, 35
United Press International: jacket, pp. 3, 4, 6–7,
   9, 19, 23, 26, 29, 30, 41, 42, 49 (bottom), 54,
   58 (both), 62, 73, 74, 89
Wide World: pp. 2, 10, 13, 15, 16, 20, 25, 37, 46,
   49 (top), 50, 60, 66, 69, 84–85, 79 (bottom), 91

Contents

Kansas City's Johnny Robinson is upended as he runs back an intercepted pass in an exciting moment of play in the 1970 Super Bowl.

They Beat the Odds

Upsets are as much a part of professional football as cleats and goalposts. Every now and then, a team that is expected to win a game does not. The underdog becomes suddenly unbeatable. Four of the most exciting upsets in pro football are described here.

"A Test for Lenny Dawson" concerns the 1970 Super Bowl. "Super Joe" is about the 1969 Super Bowl. Each game pitted the National League Football champion against the championship team in the American Football League. In both 1969 and 1970, football experts picked the National League team to win. Then the unexpected happened.

The Giants' Ken Strong kicks a field goal
in his team's win over Chicago in 1934.

"The Upstarts" tells about an earlier upset.
In 1950 the Cleveland Browns were supposedly a "weak sister" team. People laughed
and hooted when the Browns took the field
against the world champion Philadelphia
Eagles. They weren't laughing when the
final gun sounded.

"The Giants Pull a Sneaker" moves back
in time to 1934. In this upset, the underdog New York Giants used a frozen field

to their advantage in turning back the champion Chicago Bears.

Upsets are common to every sport, but particularly to football. Why? Because football is a game in which players' emotions play a major part. A team, if it can convince itself that it is the better team, can often defeat a supposedly stronger opponent. Occasionally luck sparks an upset. But almost always it is a case in which the players simply will not allow themselves to be beaten.

7

A Test for Lenny Dawson

Kansas City Chiefs vs. Minnesota Vikings
January 11, 1970

From his quarterback slot, Lenny Dawson quickly checked the positions of his Kansas City teammates. With one sweeping glance, he scanned the hulking Minnesota Viking linemen who, in an instant, would come blasting in at him.

"31, 62, 33. Hut! Hut! Hut!"

The ball snapped into Dawson's waiting hands. He darted backwards. With the swift skill that had won him the nickname "Lenny the Cool," he saw the play developing. Mike Garrett was breaking free on the left side. Dawson cocked his arm.

8

"Pass! It's a pass!" he heard a Viking linebacker bawl.

Dawson rifled the ball. Garrett grabbed it. Small and slippery, halfback Garrett gained seventeen yards. A roar from 80,988 fans threatened to shake rain from the dark clouds hanging over New Orleans' Tulane Stadium. Approximately 60 million additional people were watching on television.

Lenny Dawson prepares to pass behind the blocking of Wendell Hayes (38).

Kansas City's Stenerud boots a spectacular
48-yard field goal, scoring three points.

It was the biggest game of the year— the Super Bowl championship. The mighty Minnesota Vikings, 1969 champions of the National Football League, were being challenged by the Kansas City Chiefs, who had fought their way to the American League title.

Dawson called another pass, again on the left. This time Frank Pitts snared it. The play gained 20 yards, taking Kansas City across the 50-yard line and into the Viking territory.

On fourth down, with the ball on the Minnesota 48-yard line, Dawson signaled the bench to send in Jan Stenerud, the team's field-goal kicker. Minnesota fans sneered.

"Who does that guy think he is, trying to kick the ball that far?" asked one. "He'll miss by a mile."

But Stenerud didn't miss. He boomed the

ball between the uprights, giving Kansas City the lead, 3–0.

The Vikings took over. Standing on the sidelines, Lenny Dawson watched grimly. It was good to be in the lead, but the game was going to be a long one, just as the season had been a long and very hard one. The slim, boyish-faced Dawson was 34 years old. He had been playing football for almost as long as he could remember, but he had never had a more difficult season.

He had missed six games because of a knee injury. The knee was still painful, limiting his ability to move around and escape defensemen when they blazed in on him.

Late in the season, just two days before a crucial game against the New York Jets, Lenny's father died. Despite the tragedy, Lenny took the field and led the Chiefs to victory.

12

The camera catches Lenny Dawson in a thoughtful mood at a pre-game workout in New Orleans.

But another matter was causing Lenny real concern. Earlier in the week, a television newscaster had announced that several professional quarterbacks were to be questioned by federal officials who were investigating sports gambling. The newscaster had named Dawson as one of the quarterbacks.

No one said that Dawson had ever done any gambling. No one said that he was in

13

any way involved with gamblers. Nevertheless, the announcement that he was to be questioned had started rumors everywhere.

Dawson knew that he was expected to play a perfect game. He knew that if he threw a pass and it was caught, and the receiver scored a touchdown, the fans would cheer. But if he fumbled or threw a pass that was intercepted, the fans might shout, "Fake! Fix!" This thought tortured Lenny Dawson.

In the Minnesota Vikings, Dawson was facing the strongest defense in the National Football League. He knew he could not relax for a split second.

All week long, every time Dawson picked up a newspaper, he read words of praise for Minnesota's tough "front four." The men were ends Carl Eller and Jim Marshall, with Alan Page and Gary Larsen as tackles. Each was a mountain of a man. Their average height was 6'5", and their average weight was 260 pounds. Despite their size, each man could move with surprising quickness.

Dawson had seen films showing how the Vikings' front four had swarmed over Greg Landry, quarterback for the Detroit Lions, earlier in the season. Six times the purple-shirted marauders had broken through the

Minnesota's "front four" (left to right): Jim Marshall, Alan Page, Gary Larsen, and Carl Eller

A Minnesota defender flies through the air
as he zeros in on Kansas City quarterback
Lenny Dawson, about to fire a pass.

Detroit defense to flatten poor Landry. Their savage rushes had forced him to throw four interceptions.

Sportswriters also hailed Minnesota for its high-powered offense. Joe Kapp, the Vikings' quarterback, was husky and tough. He loved to take chances, a style in sharp contrast to Len Dawson's cool, calculating method of attack.

The newspapers gave Dawson and his teammates little chance of victory. They named the Vikings as favorites by thirteen points. However, long before the game was over, the Chiefs showed that the point spread was very wrong.

Whenever Kansas City got the ball, Lenny shredded the Minnesota defense with his pinpoint passes. Late in the first quarter, he connected with Pitts for 20 yards. He then fired to Otis Taylor for nine yards, and to Taylor again for seven yards.

The Minnesota fans were buzzing. "What's going on down there?" asked one. "How come Dawson is getting so much time to pass? Why aren't our men getting in?"

"It looks like they're double-teaming our ends, putting two men on both Eller and Marshall," a second fan answered. "Our defense can't get through."

With the ball on Minnesota's 32-yard line, Jan Stenerud came in and kicked another field goal. The Chiefs led, 6–0. Minnesota fans stared at the scoreboard in disbelief.

After the kickoff, Kapp tried to rally his team. But the Kansas City defense stopped him cold.

Again the Vikings had to punt the ball away. As Joe Kapp ran off the field, he was shaking his head.

It was first down for Kansas City on the Minnesota 44-yard line. As the Chiefs huddled, Dawson spoke, "They're driving hard

Minnesota's Bill Brown tries to escape the outstretched arms of Kansas City defenders.

up the middle with their tackles. But I think I know what to do."

Then Dawson called a play that the Chiefs referred to as "52-6-0, reverse." They had used it only twice all season.

Lenny took the snap from center. The Minnesota tackles blazed in. Dawson faked

Viking Charlie West's fumble, as it was recorded by news photographers

a handoff to his fullback heading into the line, but he gave the ball to Frank Pitts, who was running to the right. The Minnesota tackles pounced on the Kansas City fullback, while Pitts swept around the right side. The play gained nineteen yards.

Soon after, Stenerud kicked a third field goal, making the score 9–0, Kansas City.

The Vikings were beginning to feel their confidence drain away. Dawson was riddling their defenses with passes and gaining long yardage on the ground. Even when Minnesota took over the ball, they could not get a drive started.

What happened next added to the Vikings' woes. Jan Stenerud, kicking off after the field goal, sent the ball high into the air. Charlie West of the Vikings let the ball slip through his fingers. The Chiefs recovered the fumble on Minnesota's 19-yard line.

Dawson wasted no time in taking advantage of the opportunity. Coolly and deliberately, he brought the Chiefs closer and closer to the Minnesota goal.

It was first down on the Vikings' 4-yard line. Dawson handed the ball to Garrett, who lost a yard. Another running play gained nothing.

"Dawson's crazy if he thinks he can score with a running play," said one spectator. "Minnesota's given up only four touchdowns all year on the ground."

But Lenny had detected a weak spot in the Minnesota line. On the next play, Dawson assigned a blocker to open up the crack, and sent Mike Garrett through. *Touchdown!*

In the seconds after Garrett had knifed his way into the end zone, Dawson showed rare coolness. Amid the backslapping and hand-clapping, Lenny surveyed the ground

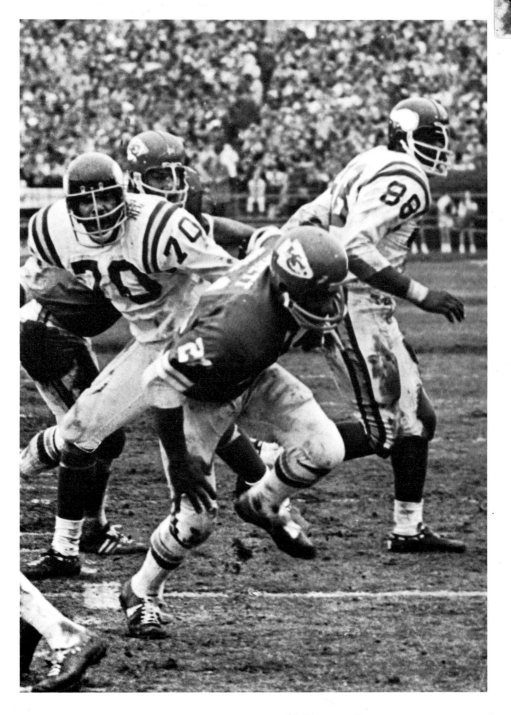

Kansas City's Mike Garrett (21) gets by two Minnesota defensemen, Jim Marshall and Alan Page, for the first touchdown.

Teammate Otis Taylor gives Mike Garrett a hug after Mike's touchdown for the Chiefs.

where the ball was to be put down for the extra-point attempt. He found it to be wet and spongy. "This could mean trouble," thought Lenny. "Stenerud might slip."

Lenny marched over to where the referee was standing. "I'd like the line of scrimmage moved back two yards," he announced. A team can decide where it wants the line of scrimmage on an extra-point try. However, the ball cannot be put down inside the opposition's 2-yard line.

24

"Okay," said the referee. He picked up the ball and stepped off the two yards.

Lenny had figured out that the adjustment would put the ball on solid turf. "Lenny the Cool" was in top-notch form. Stenerud's kick was perfect.

Kansas City held a 16–0 lead as they left the field at halftime. But Dawson knew the

Minnesota's big Joe Kapp walks dejectedly from the field.

The Vikings' Dave Osborn (41) leaps into the end zone for Minnesota's only touchdown.

job was far from finished. The Vikings were sure to fight back.

Events proved Dawson right. Late in the third quarter, the Vikings drove 69 yards for a touchdown to close within nine points of the Chiefs, 16–7.

"We've still got a chance," thought the Minnesota fans.

Dawson knew he had to strike quickly to stifle Minnesota's hopes. "Let's get that touchdown back," Dawson barked as the team huddled.

Dawson called a running play, and Mike Garrett gained five yards. He called another run, and then another. Lenny sent Wendell Hayes up the middle. Then he engineered a sweep, sending Frank Pitts around right end.

The ball was on the Minnesota 46-yard line. The Viking defense braced for another running play. But Dawson crossed them up.

He took the snap, stood erect, and fired quickly. Otis Taylor was his target. *Perfect!*

Taylor avoided one tackler and broke free of another. Then he sprinted down the right sideline for a touchdown. Stenerud booted the extra point, and Kansas City went ahead, 23–7. It was no contest after that. The Vikings fell apart.

Midway in the fourth quarter, Kapp went back to pass. He looked downfield and saw that his receivers were all covered by Kansas City defensemen. Clutching the ball to his stomach, Kapp darted to his left, hoping someone would get free. Kansas City defensemen pursued him. They caught Kapp near the sideline and pounded him to the ground. His face white with pain, Kapp was helped from the field. Some scattered boos came from the stands. Kapp had suffered a painful shoulder injury, and he played no more that day.

What was happening to the Vikings who were said to be indestructible? They were now on the brink of a smashing defeat.

Gary Cuozzo took over as quarterback for the Vikings. The alert Kansas City defense reacted to Cuozzo by intercepting one of his passes.

A few minutes later, the final gun sounded. The scoreboard read: Kansas City 23 and Minnesota 7.

Kansas City players carry Coach Stram off the field signaling that they are number one.

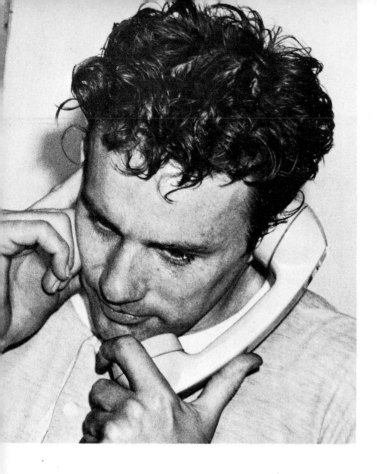

A telephone call from President Nixon for the winning team's quarterback was the icing on the cake!

Newspaper reporters mobbed Dawson in the locker room. One brought him the news that he had been voted the game's most valuable player. Then Lenny was told that the White House was calling, President Nixon wanted to talk to him. Lenny's heart pounded as he picked up the telephone. He held the receiver to his left ear, covering the other ear with his right hand to shut out the locker room clamor.

"Thank you, Mr. President, I really appreciate it," Lenny said in answer to the president's words of congratulations.

"But it wasn't me," he added. "It was the whole team that did it. I just prayed to the good Lord that I'd have the strength and courage to play a good game."

A "good" game? It was better than that. "Lenny the Cool" had been red-hot.

Super Joe

Baltimore Colts vs. New York Jets
January 12, 1969

"The Jets are going to win on Sunday. I *guarantee* it!"

This was the boast uttered to *The New York Times* by Joe Namath, the grinning, shaggy-haired quarterback of the New York Jets, just a few days before his team faced the Baltimore Colts in the 1969 Super Bowl.

Football fans were skeptical. The Jets, champions of the American Football League, were a good team, but hardly anyone believed they were a match for the mighty

Baltimore Colts, winners of the National Football League title.

The two previous Super Bowl contests were proof enough. In both, the American League team had been manhandled and badly defeated by the National League team.

Many thought that it was bound to happen again, for the Colts were looked upon as a super team. They had taken the National League championship after compiling an impressive record, winning thirteen games and losing only one. In all of football history, only three teams had ever won thirteen games in a season.

Little wonder that the Colts were favored to whip the Jets by seventeen points. Of the 55 newsmen on the scene in Miami, 49 picked Baltimore to win. One reporter predicted the final score would be: Colts 47, Jets 0.

Joe Namath speaks his mind to reporters.

Joe Namath paid no attention to the forecasts. He believed that the Jets were going to win, and he didn't mind telling newspaper reporters how he felt.

Being in the headlines was nothing new to the 25-year-old Namath. It had happened often. In 1965, following a brilliant football career at the University of Alabama, he

34

signed a reported $400,000 contract with the Jets. This was one of the highest salaries ever paid to any athlete in the United States.

But no one said that Namath was overpaid. Strong, accurate, and able to get the ball away in the blink of an eye, Namath quickly proved to be one of the finest professional passers of all time.

In the days before the 1969 Super Bowl, Namath did more than simply predict victory for his team. In an interview that appeared in *The New York Times*, he

The New York Jets' offensive line, 1969

taunted the Colts with the statement that Earl Morrall, the Baltimore quarterback, was not one of football's best.

"There are four or five quarterbacks in our league who are better than Morrall," Namath declared.

Baltimore coach Don Shula was stunned by Namath's brashness. "How can that guy put the rap on Earl?" Shula asked at a press conference a few days later.

Indeed, how could he? Morrall was a crew-cut veteran with twelve years of playing experience. He had been obtained by the Colts early in the season to fill in for quarterback Johnny Unitas, who had suffered an arm injury.

Morrall had performed brilliantly. Statistics showed him to be the NFL's no. 1 passer. In the final week of the season, he was named the National League's "Player of the Year."

**Baltimore's double threat: veteran quarter-
backs Johnny Unitas (left) and Earl Morrall**

"Namath and his loud mouth have got Baltimore fired up," said one observer. "The Colts are going to 'blitz' poor Joe to death."

Countless others agreed. The blitz—the all-out charge to flatten the quarterback—would be the weapon the Colts would use to silence Namath.

No team was better equipped for blitzing than Baltimore. Bubba Smith, their defensive left end, stood 6'7" and weighed 295 pounds. Not only was he one of the biggest players in pro football, but he was also dangerously powerful.

Mike Curtis, a Colt linebacker, had great speed, strength, and the reflexes of a tiger. Dennis Gaubatz, another linebacker and the captain of the defensive team, was a rugged, heady player.

The Colt defense had additional experience and craftiness in cornerback Bobby Boyd and daring in safety Rick Volk.

Through the regular season, it was often the defense that won the game for the Colts. In a four-game stretch, the defensive team did not allow a single touchdown. In the league championship game against the Cleveland Browns, the Colt defenders had not given up a single point. Baltimore had humiliated Cleveland, 34–0.

The Colts had a solid running game to match their bone-crushing defense. Tough Tom Matte was almost unstoppable. Jerry Hill was another dependable ground-gainer. But the team's scoring punch was in its passing. Earl Morrall could throw to a splendid trio of receivers. John Mackey, with explosive speed and power, was one of the best pass catchers in the league. Willie Richardson was wily, agile, and exceptionally fast. Jimmy Orr, a veteran, was smart and slick.

As the day of the game drew near,

Namath often repeated his boastful remarks. His bragging won him few friends, and when he trotted out onto the field that "super" Sunday, the 73,377 fans jammed into the Orange Bowl in Miami, Florida greeted him with a salvo of jeers. The quiet Morrall and the blue-shirted Colts won approving cheers.

Baltimore kicked off, and the huge crowd settled back to watch the destruction.

Earl Christy of the Jets gathered in the ball in the end zone and returned it to the 23-yard line. Namath, instead of launching an air attack as many people had expected, kept the ball on the ground. Matt Snell, the Jets' key runner, did most of the ball-carrying. Namath could not move his team beyond his own 40-yard line, and the Jets had to punt.

When Baltimore took over the ball, Morrall wasted no time in cranking up the

New York's Joe Namath (12) hands off to
Matt Snell (41) early in the game.

The Colts' "machine" was rolling smoothly when John Mackey, carrying the ball for Baltimore, was stopped by New York.

powerful Baltimore team. On Baltimore's very first play, Morrall fired to John Mackey for a 19-yard gain. Then he sent running back Tom Matte on a sweep around the right side for ten yards more.

Play after play it worked with perfection. Within five minutes, Morrall had moved the Colts to the New York 19-yard line.

The Baltimore fans were wearing smug grins as Lou Michaels came off the bench to try a field goal. Up went the ball. But it was wide—no good.

The Baltimore players shrugged. "So what," they figured. "It's early in the game. We'll get plenty of other chances."

The next opportunity came more quickly than most people expected. Late in the first quarter, the Jets fumbled. Baltimore recovered on the New York 12-yard line. Here was another golden opportunity—first down and pay dirt only twelve yards away.

Morrall called two running plays that brought the team to the New York 6-yard line. Next came a pass. Morrall took the snap from center, darted back, and cocked his arm to throw. Tom Mitchell, his target, was clear in the end zone. Morrall threw him a bullet.

But a New York defenseman flung his arms high in the air in an effort to block the pass. He tipped the ball, sending it off course. It struck Mitchell on his shoulder pads and rebounded high in the air. When it came down, Randy Beverly of the Jets was there to catch it.

The crowd gasped. Earl Morrall kicked the dirt. The Colts had been stopped a second time.

Now it was New York's ball. Namath stood over his center, bellowing the signals. He sent Matt Snell off left tackle for a gain of a yard. He called the same play again, and it got seven yards. Two more times Namath gave the ball to Snell, who raced for big gains on both attempts. Now Joe switched to the air. A pass intended for George Sauer went incomplete.

While the Jets huddled, the Colt defensive team looked at Dennis Gaubatz for a signal. "It's about time we stop this guy," Gaubatz was thinking. He gave the signal for a blitz.

The teams lined up. Namath barked his signals. The ball snapped into his hands. The Baltimore defensemen unleashed their fierce charge.

But Namath saw the blitz coming. Reacting with the quickness of a jungle cat, he fired the ball to Bill Mathis, one of his backfield men. The play earned the Jets six yards. More important, it showed that Joe Namath was quick enough to beat the blitz.

"He was lucky," said a Baltimore player. "This time let's really deck him." Gaubatz nodded in agreement.

The Colts stormed in. Again Namath got a pass away before a Baltimore player

The Jets' quarterback Joe Namath is dragged
down from behind by Baltimore's linebacker
Dennis Gaubatz in an attempt to "blitz" the
New York star.

could touch him. This time the ball went to George Sauer, and the play gained fourteen yards. The ball was now deep in the Baltimore territory. The Colt defensive team appeared to be worried.

Namath was now at his best. Again and again his lightning-quick release took the Colts by surprise. He passed to Sauer for fourteen yards and to Snell for twelve, bringing the ball within the shadow of the Baltimore goalposts.

The crowd was on its feet and screaming, but it no longer favored the Colts. They had been stirred by Namath's display of skill, by his courage and daring, and now they urged him on.

The Jets huddled. Only Namath spoke. "19-option," he said—a play in which Snell would carry the ball around the left side.

The play was executed perfectly. Snell headed left and then turned toward the

Baltimore goal. Rick Volk bolted forward to make the tackle. Suddenly, a Jet blocker chopped Volk down. Snell roared into the end zone. Jim Turner came in and kicked the extra point. Incredibly, the Jets were ahead, 7–0.

The Colts were not dead—far from it. Later in the second quarter, Baltimore penetrated to the New York 15-yard line. Morrall passed to Willie Richardson near the goalposts. But Johnny Sample of the Jets darted in front of Richardson to make an interception and kill the rally.

In the closing seconds of the first half, Baltimore was handed still another chance. From the sidelines Coach Shula sent in a play known as the "flea flicker."

Morrall took the snap from center and handed the ball to Tom Matte, who was running to his right. The Jet defense moved to tackle Matte. But before they closed in

Matt Snell (above) heads for the end zone and the first touchdown of the game. Jets' place-kicker Jim Turner boots the extra point.

**The Jets gang up on running back Jerry Hill,
the Baltimore ballcarrier.**

on him, Matte stopped in his tracks, turned,
and threw the ball back to Morrall.

It was then Morrall's task to pass to
Jimmy Orr in the end zone. The Jets had
become so bewildered by the play that they
did not have Orr covered.

Orr stood in the end zone screaming,
"Earl! Earl! Throw it! Throw it!" Morrall
failed to hear Orr, or to see him. But

50

Morrall did see Jerry Hill, another receiver, and unloaded the ball to him. But Jim Hudson of the Jets darted in front of Hill to intercept, and then the gun sounded, ending the first half.

Shula fumed at his players in the Baltimore dressing room. "You're making mistakes! You're beating yourselves!" he scolded them. "You've got them believing they're a better team than we are."

The Colts could feel the pressure as they came out for the second half. They knew they had to get some points right away.

However, it was not the Colts but the Jets who scored. Baltimore fumbled shortly after the kickoff. The Jets recovered and brought in Jim Turner to kick another field goal. The score was 10–0.

Baltimore appeared listless the next time they got the ball. They could not gain a foot, and they had to punt.

51

Earl Morrall trudged from the field, his head bowed. Coach Shula was waiting for him at the sidelines. "I'm going to take you out and put in Unitas," Shula said. Morrall did not argue. He accepted the idea. "Maybe," thought Morrall, "Unitas can get us some points."

It was New York's ball. Namath marched the Jets downfield once more. With the ball on the Baltimore 23-yard line, Namath pedaled back to pass, searching downfield for a target. Tackle Fred Miller came hurtling in and crashed into Namath just as Joe threw. The pass was short. Worse, Namath's throwing hand was injured.

The Jet quarterback hurried to the sideline, his face taut with pain. "I can't throw," he announced to Weeb Ewbank, the New York coach.

Ewbank sent Babe Parilli, the Jets' second-string quarterback, into the game.

Parilli quickly engineered another field goal.

While the team doctor for the Jets worked on Namath's injured hand, Johnny Unitas led the Colts' offensive team onto the field. Baltimore was now behind, 13–0, and needed two touchdowns to take the lead.

If any man could get the Colts the needed points, it was Johnny Unitas. Time after time in his long and brilliant career, Unitas had rescued his teammates from disaster.

Baltimore huddled. As the players listened to Unitas' firm voice, their confidence was restored. Johnny would find a way to win, they believed. Somehow he always did.

The Jet defense was not impressed by Unitas, however. They quickly forced the Colts to punt.

When the Jet offensive team came onto the field, Namath was with them. New York fans sighed with relief. Namath's injury had not proved serious.

Johnny Unitas, taking over as quarterback for Baltimore, prepares to hand off.

Once more Namath steered the Jets deep into the Baltimore territory. Jim Turner came in to kick another field goal to make the score 16–0. Now the Colts needed more than two touchdowns.

When Unitas and the Colts took over the ball, thirteen minutes and ten seconds remained in the game. "Go, Johnny, go," Colt backers chanted.

54

Unitas, his blue eyes flashing, darted back to pass. He connected with John Mackey for a five-yard gain.

Matte swept around right end for seven yards. Unitas drilled the ball to Richardson for five yards. Then Matte rushed nineteen yards for a first down on the Jets' 37-yard line. Baltimore fans took heart. At last the Colts were moving.

Cool as an iceberg, Unitas rifled the ball to Jerry Hill for a twelve-yard gain. The New York goal line was now only 25 yards away. On second down, Johnny called a pass to Jimmy Orr. Orr got loose. Unitas threw. But the ball never reached its intended target. New York's Randy Beverly knifed in front of Orr, got his hands on the ball, and wrestled it away from him.

Beverly's interception brought loud groans from the Baltimore fans. Another march had been successfully stopped.

As Namath led the New York offensive team onto the field, every eye turned to the scoreboard. The seconds were ticking away.

Namath did his job well. When Baltimore finally got the ball again, there were only six minutes and thirty-four seconds left to play. It proved enough time, however, for Unitas to kindle the Colts' hopes.

Completing one pass after another, Unitas led the Colts downfield and across the New York goal line. After the extra point was kicked, the scoreboard read: New York 16, Baltimore 7. But only three minutes and nineteen seconds remained.

The Colts were desperate. On the kickoff that followed the touchdown, Coach Shula instructed his team to try a trick play. Instead of kicking the ball deep into the New York territory, they were to attempt a short kick, hoping it would bounce off a Jet player to be recovered by a Colt.

56

The play worked! The ball, traveling low and with whistling speed, squirted out of the hands of New York's George Sauer. Tom Mitchell pounced on it for the Colts.

There was still a slim chance. What the Colts needed was another touchdown, another recovered kickoff, and then a field goal.

Could Unitas work his magic? For a brief moment it seemed he might. He connected with Willie Richardson for six yards. He hit Jimmy Orr for fourteen yards and found Willie Richardson for five yards.

Then the Jet defense stiffened. Two passes were incomplete. It was fourth down for the Colts on the New York 19-yard line. Five yards were needed for a first down.

Unitas called a pass. With Jimmy Orr as his target, Unitas fired. Larry Grantham, a Jet linebacker, reached up and knocked the ball to the ground.

A happy ending for
Joe Namath (left)
and his teammates
surrounding Coach
Weeb Ewbank.

The Colt situation was hopeless now. The clock showed that two minutes and twenty-one seconds remained. Namath would be able to sew up the game by calling running plays. And that is what he did.

When the Colts did get the ball back, only eight seconds were left. Namath stood at the sidelines and watched the scoreboard clock count off the final seconds—four, three, two, one. As the gun sounded, a broad grin crossed Namath's face.

Then he turned and hurried toward the Jet dressing room. Tears of joy welled up in his eyes. As he ran, Namath thrust his right hand above his head and extended his index finger to signal that the Jets were the no. 1 team in professional football. He had always believed that they were. By fashioning one of the most astonishing upsets in football history, he had made believers out of the whole world.

**Otto Graham was the Cleveland Browns' star
quarterback in their first NFL game.**

The Upstarts

Cleveland Browns vs. Philadelphia Eagles
September 16, 1950

Otto Graham winced as if in pain. The boos and hisses thundered down from the stands at Philadelphia's Municipal Stadium. This was a new experience for Otto, a veteran of four seasons as quarterback for the Cleveland Browns.

"The Browns are nothing but cheesecake champs," Otto heard someone bellow. "Tonight they're going to play *real* professionals."

The Browns huddled. Graham called the play—a pass. He took the snap from center

61

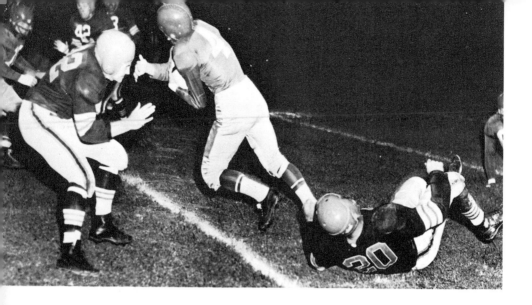

The Browns managed to stop the Eagles, as
in this first-quarter tackle of Philadelphia
halfback Frank Ziegler.

and drifted back to throw. But his receivers
were covered by the alert defensemen of
the Philadelphia Eagles. One leaped high in
the air to bat the ball to the ground.

On the next play, Graham tried another
pass. Again it was stopped.

"Back to the bush league, Otto," came a
fan's taunt.

Graham wore a mask of grim determina-
tion as the players huddled. He could not
remember a time when he had wanted so

much to win a game. But already the contest was developing into an uphill struggle for his team. Midway in the first quarter, a Philadelphia field goal had put the Eagles ahead, 3–0.

Once more Graham went back to throw. A hulking Philadelphia lineman hurtled toward him. Graham cooly sidestepped the charge.

Far downfield, Otto spotted receiver Dub Jones, and he lofted a long spiral in his direction. Jones, galloping at full speed, made a desperate lunge, grabbed the ball in the clear, and sprinted 25 yards into the Philadelphia end zone. *Touchdown!* Lou Groza came in and kicked the extra point. Cleveland led, 7–3. The Philadelphia fans sat in stunned silence.

As Otto trotted to the sidelines, he permitted himself a brief smile. "Not bad for a 'bush league' team," he thought.

The "bush league" was the All America Conference, a league that operated from 1946 through 1949. In those four years the Browns won the conference championship each season.

In January 1950, after the signing of a merger agreement with the National Football League, the All America Conference was dissolved, and the Browns were taken into the NFL. The National League teams were much more experienced.

Football fans could hardly wait for Cleveland's first game in National League competition. "The 'big boys' will give those upstarts a lesson in football," said one observer.

For Cleveland's first opponents in National League play, officials had arranged the sternest challengers possible—the Philadelphia Eagles. The Eagles had won the National League championship in 1948 and again in 1949. They were considered the best team in pro football.

The Eagles had rugged linemen in end Pete Pihos and tackle Al Wistert. Their center Alex Wojciechowicz had first won fame as a "block of granite" at Fordham University. They had one of football's best quarterbacks in Tommy Thompson, a dead-eyed passer. Philadelphia's pile-driving running back, Steve Van Buren, had been injured and would not play. But his substitute, the speedy Clyde (Smackover) Scott, was a man of proven ability and skill.

Cleveland had its own array of stars, but none was brighter than Otto Graham. Otto, from Waukegan, Illinois, was a born athlete. He was strong, well-coordinated, and he had a delicate sense of rhythm and timing. More important, he owned a deep sense of pride and a fiery competitive spirit.

In high school, Otto won letters in track, basketball, and football. Later, at Northwestern University in Evanston, Illinois, he starred in basketball and football.

After he joined the Browns, Graham's trademark became the long pass. He could toss the ball half the length of the football field with remarkable accuracy. He would

Coach Paul Brown, in his usual baseball hat, discusses some plays with team members.

arch the ball high in the air so that it settled light as a feather into the arms of the receiver. Otto was skilled in throwing short passes too. These he fired with bullet speed.

Graham had two sure-handed receivers in Mac Speedie and Dante Lavelli. Lavelli, with his blazing speed, was at his best when the pressure was greatest. Speedie was more of a trickster.

The Brown's running game was built around the talents of Marion Motley, a fullback with the power and drive of an army tank.

Together the players functioned as a well-oiled machine. In their four years of competition in the All America Conference, the Browns had won 52 games, tied 3, and lost only 4.

Despite this incredible record, virtually every person in the crowd of 71,237 who turned out to watch the Browns in their National League debut believed they would be humiliated by the Eagles.

As the second quarter opened, the Eagles started their own attack. They marched downfield, penetrating deep into the Cleveland territory. Then Philadelphia fumbled the ball on the Cleveland 25-yard line, and the Browns recovered.

A short time later, Philadelphia got a second drive under way. It carried them to the Cleveland 2-yard line. "Go! Go! Go!" shrieked the Eagles' fans. But the Browns defended their goal fiercely, and the Eagles could not make a touchdown.

The Browns took over the ball. The team huddled. "It's time we started using some sideline passes," Graham said.

The sideline pass was Cleveland's deadliest weapon. As Graham took the snap from center, Lavelli and Speedie darted two

Dante Lavelli, end, Cleveland Browns

or three steps downfield. Lavelli turned
abruptly and streaked for the left sideline;
Speedie broke in the opposite direction. Otto
would then fire to one or the other just
before the man went out of bounds.

The sideline pass was agony for the
Philadelphia defense. They were not able to
stop it.

Graham moved the Browns all the way to
the Eagles' 26-yard line. Coach Paul Brown

69

sent in a play from the bench. It was to be another pass to Speedie.

Following instructions, Graham went back to throw, with Speedie as his intended target. But out of the corner of his eye, Graham saw the other end, Lavelli, far behind the Philadelphia defense and racing toward pay dirt.

Graham whipped the ball to Lavelli, and the Browns had another touchdown. The score was 14–3 as the teams left the field at halftime.

In the Philadelphia locker room, Coach Greasy Neale addressed his players. "Don't worry," he said. "We'll get these guys. There's plenty of time left."

"But we've got to stop those sideline passes," he added. "We're going to have to start rushing Graham. We're going to have to dump him before he has a chance to get the ball away."

70

In the third quarter, it seemed as though the Eagles' new strategy might work. By rushing Graham, the Eagles stifled the Cleveland passing attack—for a time.

Coach Brown knew how to combat the new defense. He told Marion Motley, the big fullback, to stay back with Otto and to block for him. "Keep those guys away from Graham," the coach instructed.

Marion Motley, a fullback for the Cleveland Browns

That is exactly what Motley did. Whenever one of the Eagles broke through the Cleveland forward line, Motley was waiting to bowl the man over.

Graham got another march under way early in the third period. Mixing snappy short passes with long floaters, he took the Browns to the Philadelphia 13-yard line.

Then Otto missed a pass and called another. As Graham stood poised to pass, Norm Willey of the Eagles crashed through the Cleveland defense and evaded Motley. He got his arms around Otto, but Graham broke free. He had spotted Speedie in the clear and hit him with a touchdown pass. After Groza kicked the extra point, Cleveland held a 21–3 lead.

The Philadelphia fans could not believe their eyes. This was no "minor league" team they were watching. The Browns were hard-rock pros.

Hal Herring, Cleveland Brown center, intercepts a pass and breaks into the open.

Late in the third quarter, the Eagles intercepted one of Graham's tosses and turned it into a touchdown. After the Eagles booted the extra point, the score was 21–10.

Within a matter of minutes, Graham again smashed Philadelphia's flickering hopes. He shifted from a passing game to a ground attack. On play after play, he sent Marion Motley, Dub Jones, or Rex Bumgardner sweeping around the ends.

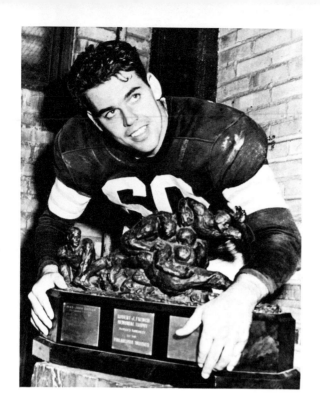

Otto Graham takes the trophy as best player in the win over Philadelphia.

This change in strategy produced two more touchdowns for Cleveland. When the gun sounded, ending the game, the scoreboard showed the Browns on top, 35–10.

Graham and the Browns left the playing field with the warm applause of the spectators ringing in their ears. Yet despite their great victory, the Browns did not gloat.

"Were the teams in All America Conference tougher than the Eagles?" a reporter asked Otto.

Graham grinned. "Any team is tough to beat," he said.

What Graham and the Browns did to the Eagles was no accident. The team ended the season with ten wins and only two losses, and turned back the Los Angeles Rams in the National League championship play-off.

As for Graham himself, he went on to establish a unique record. In each of the ten seasons he played professional football —four in the All America Conference and six in the National Football League—he led the Cleveland Browns to a football title. No other quarterback in pro football history has ever operated with such perfection.

But it was that Saturday night in September 1950 in Philadelphia's Municipal Stadium that Graham and his teammates first showed they could whip the "big boys."

The Giants Pull a Sneaker

New York Giants vs. Chicago Bears
December 9, 1934

Stout, red-faced Steve Owen, coach of the New York Giants, stared out of the window of his hotel room at the bleak December sky, his brow wrinkled with worry.

In just a few hours, Owen's team was to face the rugged Chicago Bears in the play-off game that would decide the championship of the National Football League.

The Giants, handicapped by injuries, were given little chance. Indeed, Owen himself had stopped believing that the Giants could win. "How badly are we going to get beaten?" was what he kept thinking.

Owen's thoughts that cheerless December morning were suddenly interrupted by the ring of the telephone. It was Jack Mara, one of the owners of the New York team. He was calling from the nearby Polo Grounds, where the game was to be played.

"I called to tell you the field is frozen," Mara said. "It's as hard as ice."

Owen sighed. The frozen field just added to his problems.

Harry Newman, New York's quarterback and ace passer, had previously suffered a pair of cracked ribs and would be out of action. A young rookie named Ed Danowski, normally a halfback, would have to replace him. An untried rookie at the quarterback slot in a championship game? Owen had no other choice.

The Giants' Stuart Clancy, a back, and

Morris (Red) Badgro, an end, were also sidelined. With their best players injured, the Giants were going to have to face one of the most powerful football machines of all time.

The Bears had blazed through the 1934 season unbeaten and untied. They boasted a winning streak of 33 games.

The Giants' season record showed eight wins against five losses, and two of the defeats had come at the hands of the Bears.

Chicago's striking power was partly due to the size of their players. They outweighed the Giants on an average of twelve pounds a man in the line, and fifteen pounds a man in the backfield.

The Giants had no player to equal Chicago's big Bronko Nagurski, the man who would lead the Bears' attack. With a barrel chest and legs like tree trunks, he was the most feared ballcarrier of the day.

The Giants faced
strong opposition
from the Bears'
Bronko Nagurski
(right) and Jack
Manders (below).

The Bears also had "automatic" Jack Manders, a place-kick specialist. He was capable of booting a field goal from anywhere inside the 50-yard line.

Just a year before, the Giants had been defeated by the Bears through a freak play in the championship play-off. The players wanted revenge for this loss. Now the day for revenge had come, but the Giants were in no shape to hand out punishment to anyone.

When Owen went to the dining room for breakfast, he reported the frozen playing conditions to end Ray Flaherty and tackle Bill Morgan.

Flaherty, who was team captain, said, "You know we might be able to make this work to our advantage."

Owen's brow wrinkled. "What do you mean?" he asked in his flat Oklahoma drawl.

80

"We could wear sneakers," said Flaherty.

"Sneakers?" said Owen.

"Yes, sneakers," Flaherty said. "Listen, when I was at Gonzaga University, we once played Montana State on a frozen field. Someone came up with the bright idea of having us wear rubber-bottomed sneakers instead of football cleats. The Montana players slipped around like seals on a cake of ice, and we ran circles around them."

Owen shrugged. "It might work," he said.

"I *know* it will," said Bill Morgan. "I saw Washington University use sneakers on a frozen field in a game against the Seattle All Stars. Do you know what the score was at halftime? Washington led, 69–0."

"Okay, let's try it," Owen said.

But there was a problem. Where could Owen get enough sneakers to outfit his team? Since it was Sunday, sporting goods stores and gymnasiums were closed.

When Owen arrived at the Polo Grounds, he called the coaches and players together. "Does anyone know where we can get some sneakers?" he asked.

An assistant trainer named Abe Cohen spoke up. "A friend of mine knows the basketball coach at Manhattan College. He'd let us borrow the team's basketball sneakers."

"Great!" said Owen. "Get a taxi and go and get them."

Game time was nearing as Abe Cohen set out for Manhattan College. The Giants pulled on their regulation cleated shoes and trotted out onto the field. The temperature had dropped to nine degrees, and the gridiron was concrete-hard.

Whipped by an icy wind, the brave fans huddled in small clusters. Some wore overshoes, boots, or heavy stockings over their shoes, and many wrapped blankets around their legs. Scarfs or stocking caps covered their heads—anything to keep from freezing.

Then the game started. Spearheaded by Danowski's short passing attack and the running of Ken Strong, New York drove to the Chicago 7-yard line.

It was first down, and the ball went to Danowski, who intended to follow Strong's blocking. But Strong slid and fell on a patch of ice. In poured the Chicago defense on the unfortunate Danowski, throwing him for an eight-yard loss.

The goal line was now fifteen yards away. Danowski did not think that a run would work. He called a pass, but it was intercepted. Chicago took over the ball.

Four plays later, the Giants broke through the Chicago defenses and blocked a punt, recovering the ball on the Bears' 30-yard line. Strong then booted a field goal to give the New Yorkers a 3–0 lead.

The next time the Bears got the ball, the
tide of battle began to swing in their favor.

The slippery footing did not seem to
hinder Nagurski or his teammate Keith
Molesworth. They took turns ripping wide
holes in the New York line. Nobody could
stop Nagurski as he butted his way into
the Giants' end zone for the game's first

84

Chicago quarterback Keith Molesworth, about to smother a fumbled ball in the first quarter

touchdown. Jack Manders booted the extra point. Chicago led, 7–3.

Steve Owen, pacing the sidelines to keep warm, shook his head grimly.

After the kickoff, the Giants were unable to move the ball and had to punt. Nagurski and Molesworth raced through the Giant line for 44 yards in two plays and set up a field goal. Into the game came Jack Manders. His kick was perfect. The Bears led, 10–3.

Minutes later, the first half ended. The bigger Bears had given the Giants a rough time, and Owen's charges limped from the field, weary and discouraged.

Some of the Giants slouched on locker room benches. Others stretched out on the concrete floor. The room was silent.

Suddenly the dressing room door burst open. There stood Abe Cohen, arms loaded with sneakers.

"I've got nine pairs!" he exclaimed. "All I could carry." He dumped them in a pile on the dressing room floor.

"Put them on," shouted Steve Owen. "Hurry! We don't have much time."

Tackle Bill Owen was the first to don the

sneakers. He trotted out of the dressing room door and came back grinning.

"You know, they feel pretty good," he said. "Maybe we've got a chance."

When the Giants filed out onto the field for the second half, the fans were puzzled by what they saw.

"What are they wearing?" said one. "Do they think this is a basketball game?" asked another.

A Chicago player pointed out the rubber-soled footwear to George Halas, the Chicago coach. Halas was not impressed.

"That's okay," he said. "Step on their toes."

The sneakers were not effective immediately. The Giants fumbled and Chicago recovered. This opened the way for Manders to boot another field goal. Chicago led, 13–3.

"That's the last nail in the coffin," said a frozen fan. "I've seen enough." Hundreds of other spectators agreed and began to make their way to the exit gates.

Then, minutes before the third quarter ended, the Giants started to roll, thanks to their sneakers. Their pass receivers found that the rubber soles helped them elude the Chicago defensemen. Danowski completed pass after pass, bringing the New Yorkers to within scoring range.

Danowski called another pass. He spotted end Ike Frankian near the Chicago goal line. The New York substitute quarterback fired. Chicago's Carl Brumbaugh raced toward Frankian, intent on making the interception. Brumbaugh, leaping high, managed to get his hands on the ball, but Frankian tore it away and dashed into the end zone for New York's first touchdown.

Ken Strong kicked the extra point for New York. Now the score was 13–10. The Chicago lead was cut to three points.

**Two Giants' players try to stop big Bronko
Nagurski from running to daylight.**

The Giants were fired up. They knew
that in order to win, they were going to
have to stop Bronko Nagurski—and they
did! Whenever big Bronko carried the ball,
the sneaker-footed Giants were able to reach
him before he could get up speed. Time

after time they pounded him to the ground.

Unable to advance the ball, the Bears punted. The New York defense surged in, forcing the Chicago kicker to hurry. It was a poor punt, slicing out of bounds on the Chicago 48-yard line. Now it was New York's ball.

Steve Owen had stationed Lou Little, the Columbia University football coach, in the stands to spot Bear weaknesses. Little noticed that the Giants could outrun the Bears on plays that went to the outside, toward either of the sidelines. He telephoned the information to Owen.

Owen beckoned to Danowski. "Try a run with Strong down the right side," he said.

The ball went to Strong. He tore straight toward the center of the line. The Chicago defense braced to stop him. Strong then faked to his left, but cut sharply to his right.

With his sneakers gripping the frozen field, Strong flashed down the sideline. Two burly Bears began to close in, but Strong danced right by them. He never stopped running until he reached the goal line.

The New York fans went wild. Hundreds of them poured out of the stands and surrounded the playing field.

Ken Strong won the day for the New York Giants.

They sent up loud cheers as Strong kicked the extra point, putting the Giants ahead, 17–13. Steve Owen grinned—for the first time that day.

The Bears were in a state of shock. All year long no team had scored more than sixteen points against them. Now in the space of a few short minutes, the Giants had scored *seventeen.*

Time was running out. The Bears knew they had to rally. But they could not get a drive under way and had to give up the ball again.

The Giants called a reverse. Danowski took the snap from center and started running to his left, then deftly handed the ball to Ken Strong, who was circling in the opposite direction. The Chicago players were unable to make the sudden change in direction. Several skidded and fell. Strong romped across the goal line.

A reverse was considered impossible on a frozen field. But with sneakers *nothing* was impossible. The Giants were ahead, 23–13.

Dazed and disappointed, the Bears would not give up. Chicago halfback Gene Ronzani went back to pass. The New York defenders tore through the Bears' line. Ronzani had to hurry his throw, and the Giants intercepted.

Two plays later, just before time ran out, Danowski swooped across the Chicago goal line without a hand touching him. The final score was 30–13.

The Giants staged one of the most stunning comebacks in football history. In the last fifteen minutes of play, they scored 27 points.

Fans swarmed onto the field. They broke down the wooden goalposts and splintered them for souvenirs.

The Chicago dressing room was a dismal scene. Many players wept.

"They won it with the sneakers," said Bronko Nagurski bitterly. "They could run and cut. We couldn't."

Carl Brumbaugh sat on a bench, staring at the floor. "Halas told us to step on their toes," he said. "I couldn't get close enough to step on anybody's toes."

New York had many heroes, but most of the sportswriters singled out Ken Strong as the game's outstanding player. With his lightning runs for touchdowns and with his sure-footed kicks, Strong had scored seventeen points.

In the joy-filled Giants' locker room, scores of people crowded about Strong to congratulate him. One was Abe Cohen. "Great game, Ken," said Cohen, pumping Strong's hand. "You were terrific."

"I can't take much credit," Strong said.

"If Owen hadn't decided to use sneakers, it would have been a different ball game."

"But, you know, Abe," Strong added with a big grin, "you're the man who really won this game."

Abe Cohen's name did not appear in the newspaper accounts of the game. It can't be found in any record book. But true Giant fans will never forget Abe Cohen and his hurried mission to Manhattan College.